Wedding Toasts & Vows

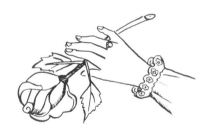

Wedding Toasts & Vows

Bette Matthews

FRIEDMAN/FAIRFAX
PUBLISHERS

A FRIEDMAN/FAIRFAX BOOK

Please visit our website: www.metrobooks.com

© 2001 by Michael Friedman Publishing Group, Inc.

Library of Congress Cataloging-in-Publication Data

Matthews, Bette.
   Toasts and vows / Bette Matthews.
      p. cm.
   ISBN 1-58663-121-7 (alk. paper)
    1. Marriage service. 2. Wedding toasts. 3. Vows. I. Title.

BL619.M37 M38 2001
392.5—dc21

2001018763

Editor: Dan Heend
Art Director: Jeff Batzli
Designer: Kirsten Berger
Illustrations © Kirsten Berger
Production Manager: Rosy Ngo

Printed in Spain by Book Print, S.L.

1 3 5 7 9 10 8 6 4 2

Distributed by Sterling Publishing Company, Inc.
387 Park Avenue South
New York, NY 10016
Distributed in Canada by Sterling Publishing
Canadian Manda Group
One Atlantic Avenue, Suite 105
Toronto, Ontario, Canada M6K 3E7
Distributed in Australia by
Capricorn Link (Australia) Pty Ltd.
P.O. Box 6651
Baulkham Hills, Business Centre, NSW 2153, Australia

To my husband, Antonio:
Here's to us, joined in every quadrant.

Acknowledgments

The author would like to thank the Reverend James Wentz,
Rabbi Carie Carter, Father Bob, and James Strickland
for their kind cooperation and generous donations of time and knowledge.
I would also like to thank the following people for contributing a piece of
their lives to this volume, and granting permission to reproduce their
gracious words: Carol Guasti and Jean Miele, Jerianne Ritchie, Annie Morse
and Kevin Pierce, Ron Deutsch, Kerry and George Vaughan,
Antonio M. Rosario, Maxine Dormer, and Maya Shea and Jack Wan.

Contents

My heartiest congratulations to you. If you are reading this book, chances are that you will soon make a lifelong commitment to your beloved. For most, this means a marriage ceremony, be it religious, traditional, civil, unconventional, or even one not recognized by any authority other than your own hearts. Whether you have been designing this moment in your imagination for years or have never given it a second thought, you are now faced with the task of planning your wedding. Your marriage ceremony is the most important part of this event: the occasion's purpose and the element that gives meaning to the celebration. There are many ways to get married, and the only "right" way is to discover what is meaningful to you. Decisions regarding your ceremony should be determined by both bride and groom together, for marriage is a major undertaking and should be entered into with more than just consent. Responsibility, collaboration, anticipation, intent, and interest will all be required throughout your marriage. What better way to start your married life than planning this first step together?

Essential Elements

There are only two aspects of the wedding ceremony that must be included for your marriage to be recognized as legally binding by the federal government. Your vows, or promises to each other, acknowledge your willing consent and commitment to enter into this union. Typically, this is the familiar section that takes some form of "Do you take this man/woman to be your lawfully wedded wife/husband?" and so on, and the response "I do." However, the words themselves can be anything of your choosing, as long as the intent is the same. The second condition for a minimalist wedding is the declaration by a recognized authority of the state that you are now "husband and wife."

Wedding Wisdom

There are many legal requirements regarding marriage. These vary from state to state, and include restrictions on who may marry, who may perform the ceremony, number of witnesses needed, and requisite licenses and blood tests involved. Check with your local marriage bureau or county clerk to obtain the guidelines for your region.

The traditional wedding, on the other hand, is rich in the symbols of faith and heritage, and generally follows a format defined by a house of worship. This may include rituals common to the faith and not specific to the marriage ceremony, such as the Catholic practice of receiving communion at a nuptial mass.

By marrying in this environment, you are committing your relationship to a larger belief system, as well as its ideals about marriage and family. While the opportunities for personalizing a religious wedding may be fewer, with more restrictions imposed, they do exist, and for those of you with deep religious or ethnic affiliations, this type of ceremony will have the most meaning. Even if you are not planning a religious wedding, you might choose the formal structure of the traditional wedding ceremony as the basis for your vows. The familiarity of this type of service provides a sense of community, history, and continuity for participants and guests alike.

Wedding Wisdom

If a five-minute wedding rite with only the bare necessities spoken is your style, don't feel you have to change it. This might be the perfect ceremony for you, but it should be a decision, *not a default.*

If you opt to travel a nontraditional route, there are worlds of options for making your ceremony quintessentially unique. You will find that crafting your vows with your future spouse will be an emotionally bonding experience, one in which you can pick and choose the symbols and rituals that are meaningful to you, creating a sense of community and family in your own way and inventing your own wedding customs.

Your ceremony is a solemn event, in that it is profound, awe-inspiring, and significant—but this does not mean that it has to be stern. Approach it with pomp and ritual if that is your style, or with dignified earnestness, or even with lighthearted informality, if that best reflects your personalities—but remember to approach it with the respect it deserves.

Constructing Your Ceremony

You have determined the tone, be it formal, religious, mystical, unconventional, playful, or casual. Think about the underlying structure as your building block. The following parts of the wedding ceremony reflect a fairly common order of service.

WELCOME

Also called the opening words, this is the beginning of your ceremony and immediately follows the procession. Here your officiant will greet the assembly, reminding everyone why you are gathered together. He or she may choose to offer a sermon, teaching, or prayer as well, perhaps about the meaning of love, marriage, and community.

READINGS

You or an honored participant read selected prose, poetry, or religious passages. You can choose one or several readings, placed in the same section of the ceremony or scattered throughout the service. In a religious service the readings might have to be biblical in origin. In a nontraditional service, you may draw your readings from unusual sources, such as the "What is Real?" section from *The Velveteen Rabbit*, Edward Lear's poem *The Owl and the Pussycat*, or lyrics from a contemporary love song.

Question of Intent

In this part of a traditional service, the bride may be presented for marriage by her father or parents, and you both will be questioned about your intent to marry of your own free will. In some ceremonies, this section is combined with the vows. This is also the section in which congregants are asked if anyone can give reason why you should not be wed.

Vows

The most personal part of the service and the greatest opportunity for speaking from the heart, the vows are the pledges you make to each other for the future. In some religious ceremonies you may not have the option to personalize the vows, but most allow it. For a nontraditional service, this is a wonderful opportunity to write your own vows and speak your innermost hopes and promises.

Exchange of Rings

Here, the groom places the wedding band on the bride's finger. If you are having a double ring ceremony, the bride also places the groom's wedding band on

his finger. This can take place with or without spoken words. In a religious wedding, the cleric will usually bless the rings before the exchange.

Blessing

This is generally a part of a religious wedding, asking for God's support of the marriage. It can be a very personal moment, if your officiant chooses to speak so that only the bride and groom can hear the words. The blessing can also be offered for the entire congregation, and may even be made by a relative or friend.

Declaration

The celebrant pronounces to all that you are now husband and wife.

Closing Words

This can take the form of a prayer, blessing, benediction, or statement of hope and good will for the future.

Making It Personal

There are as many marriage ceremonies as there are religious denominations, ethnic cultures, and unique individuals in this world. When crafting your ceremony, choose rites, symbols, and customs that resonate with your spiritual, emotional, and cultural selves. Be aware that ethnic traditions can often be particularly moving. In various Asian cultures, for example, the sipping of wine or sake replaces spoken vows. There is an Italian custom of offering flowers and prayers to the Virgin Mary, as well as a beautiful Ukrainian crowning ceremony. Some Native American nations sanctify a space with a purification ritual called smudging, and jumping the broom has become an African-American tradition in the United States. In the Quaker wedding ceremony there is no officiant, and the bride and groom basically marry themselves.

Wedding Wisdom

Rituals should only be incorporated into your wedding if they have true significance for you. A showy display of unrelated practices used only for the sake of making your ceremony appear glamorous or unusual will, in actuality, seem hollow and out of place.

Music is also a wonderful means of putting your personal stamp on the marriage ceremony. Some houses of worship have restrictions regarding the use of secular music, but many allow it. Hymns are always appropriate, and other classics range from *Ave Maria* to *Trumpet Voluntary* to Pachelbel's *Canon in D* to a selection from *The Four Seasons.* Many a bride would feel cheated if she didn't enter to Wagner's *Bridal Chorus,* or exit to Mendelsohn's *Wedding March.* For a more modern take, consider music from Enya, Andreas Vollenweider, or Vangelis. *The Wedding Song* is charming for a musical interlude, as is *What a Wonderful World, Can You Feel the Love Tonight,* or *Love Me Tender.*

Other ceremonies can be added to your order of service, such as the lighting of a unity candle. Often, a chosen musical piece fills in the background of this ritual. Two individual tapers are lit and held by the bride and groom. Next, they light a central taper or pillar candle together, using their individual candles to signify the joining of their lives. Some choose to extinguish the individual flames, leaving only the central candle burning. Others appreciate the significance of allowing individuality to remain intact. Add a special touch to this ceremony by having your parents light the individual candles for you.

The Rose Ceremony is also gaining in popularity. In this ritual, the bride and groom each exchange a single red rose, symbol of love. The celebrant explains that although there are no outward signs that anything has occurred, the bride and groom have both freely given and accepted a token of their commitment to each other. They are reminded that days will stretch before them in which life may seem ordinary, but they must always remember to build their enduring relationship on the mutual exchange of love.

Here are a few more ideas for personalizing your service:

1. Rather than "giving away the bride" in the traditional way, have your celebrant ask your parents or the congregation "Who will support and encourage this couple in the commitment they are about to make?" The correct response, of course, is "We do!"

2. Have a member of the wedding party pass your rings to all present for a blessing.

3. If one or both of you have children, include them in the ceremony. Allow your child to present you to the marriage, or include additional vows and a ring ceremony for the child.

4. Incorporate a wine ceremony into the celebration, whereby you hold a chalice to each other's lips to drink.

5. Add a handfasting ceremony, in which both partners' hands are bound together with a piece of red fabric until after the ceremonial kiss, symbolizing the physical and spiritual bonding of the two.

6. Ask a trusted friend or family member to choose a reading appropriate for your wedding and surprise you with it during the ceremony.

The following sections present ideas for appropriate vows for various types of wedding ceremonies, and are by no means comprehensive in nature. Rather, in each you will find inspiration for personalizing your service, with examples from truly special weddings.

Religious Weddings

For a religious wedding, it is important to discuss the service with your clergy member, in order to understand how a marriage is celebrated in that particular house of worship and what options you have for personalizing it. In the Jewish wedding there are at least two wonderful opportunities to personalize your vows. During the betrothal section, or *Erusin*, the groom places the wedding ring on the bride's forefinger, reciting in Hebrew words that translate as *"Behold, you are hereby consecrated unto me with this ring in accordance with the law of Moses and the people of Israel."* If there is to be a double ring ceremony, the bride then places a wedding ring on the groom's finger, speaking her choice of words, such as *"I am my beloved's and my beloved is mine,"* or *"I betroth you unto me forever,"* or *"Set me as a seal upon thine heart, as a seal upon thine arm."* During this section, many rabbis welcome the couple to offer words from their hearts. Here is a beautiful example:

Deborah, I make these lifelong promises to you: I will love you and be faithful to you, I will stand by your side in darkness and in light, I will lift you up when I am strong, and lean on you when I am not. I will build a family with you and teach our children to value the things we hold precious in life. God set our souls aside for each other before we were born. I give you this ring, and will wear mine proudly, as a symbol of our love, which has no beginning and will never end. From this day forth, you are my cherished wife.

Another opportunity for personalized vows arises when the rabbi reads the *ketubah* (the marriage contract) aloud. A conventional *ketubah* has traditional wording in Aramaic, outlining the man's responsibility to the woman in marriage. Many couples choose to have a second, egalitarian *ketubah* reflecting the responsibilities they feel to each other and the promises they make together in marriage. An example of this type is shown below in the section on interfaith weddings.

In a Catholic wedding, the exchange of vows can take either of two forms. In the question format, the priest will ask, *"[Groom's name], do you take [bride's name] to be your wife? Do you promise to be true to her in good times and in bad, in sickness and in health, to love her and honor her all the days of your life?"* The groom responds, *"I do."* In the statement format, the priest will prompt you to make the following declaration, *"I, [groom], take you, [bride], to be my wife. I promise to be true to you in good times and in bad, in sickness and in health. I will love you and honor you all the days of my life."*

Another traditional wording is, *"[Groom], do you take [bride] for your lawful wife, to have and to hold, from this day forward, for better, for worse, for richer, for poorer, in sickness and in health, till death do you part?"*

Many nuances and variations of the wedding vows are found in the different Protestant denominations. Based on the matrimonial rites in the *Book of Common Prayer*, you are instructed to hold your partner's right hand in yours, and say, *"In the name of God, I, [groom], take you, [bride], to be my wife, to have and to hold from this day forward, for better or for worse, for richer or for poorer, in sickness and in health, to love and to cherish, until we are parted by death. This is my solemn vow."*

If your church permits personalized vows, it will still be important to express the same commitments that are found in the conventional ritual, as in these touching words:

On this most joyous day before God and our community, I, Catherine, choose to enter into the partnership of holy matrimony with you, Daniel, forsaking all others. I promise to love, comfort, and protect you with all that I am, to respect, cherish, and encourage you always. I will live according to God's plan for us, and face all the challenges of life with you. I will share the joys, endure the difficulties, and circumvent any obstacle in our path. I make this solemn vow of commitment to you, for as long as we both shall live.

Remember that your priest or minister must approve any deviation from the standard text.

In the case of an interfaith wedding, you are often encouraged to customize your ceremony by choosing parts from both religious ceremonies, focusing on those that most resonate with your relationship. Perhaps you will choose to marry under a *chuppah*, share a *sas-san-kudo* sake ceremony, include readings both biblical and secular, exchange the sign of peace, or have both officiants offer traditional blessings. You may personalize your vows to reflect your diverse backgrounds, as in the case of these promises, which begin with the lighting of a unity candle and end with the exchange of rings:

The groom and bride light individual candles in turn, saying:

>   [Ellen/Christopher], I have chosen you as the one [woman/man] in all the world that I wish to share my life with, and rejoice that you have chosen me. I light this candle for all to witness my willingness to enter into wedlock with you.

>   Together the bride and groom use their candles to light a central candle, and the groom says: Today we combine our individual light to create something new and unique, something that is more than each of us alone.

The bride says:

>   We place our burning candles on either side of this new light, to watch over it each with our own energy. We are one, we are two, we are three unique forces at once.

The couple exchanges vows, each in turn:

I, [Christopher/Ellen], commit my life to you, [Ellen/Christopher] in marriage with all the love that resides within my heart. I promise to love you for who you are, wholly and fully, in good fortune and adversity alike, in this life and beyond.

The ring exchange:

With this ring, I thee wed, in the name of the Father, and of the Son, and of the Holy Spirit, amen.

Be sanctified unto me with this ring in keeping with the heritage of Moses and Israel.

The Jewish tradition of the *ketubah,* or marriage contract, can be particularly meaningful when written by the couple:

In accordance with both of our beliefs and as witnessed by our families and friends, we hereby declare our everlasting commitment to each other and to our marriage. We promise to keep the love and hope of this day ever present in our consciousness, and remember those feelings when conflicts arise. We promise to search for new ways to blend our diverse backgrounds to create something new, without losing the old. We accept that compromise and sacrifice go hand in hand with growth and development, and we vow to embrace our diversity and thereby enrich our lives, open our minds, and help us to grow beyond what we are presently. We resolve to search for solutions to our unique trials together, solutions in which we can both feel peace and know that one has not triumphed at the expense of the other.

We will be the refuge for each other, the stable force, the norm by which all else will be judged. We will approach each other with compassion, respect, and devotion, encourage each other's individuality without giving up our own and without forfeiting our partnership. With all that we are and all that we have, we make this sacred covenant today in front of these witnesses.

Contemporary Vows

Although they wrote the service themselves, the ceremony of George and Kerry had a sonorous, traditional air. Their celebrant was a close friend, who spoke of the dreams binding the couple together, their unique personalities and spirits, and the importance of cherishing every moment given to us, as the nature of life is temporary. Facing each other and holding hands, the bride and groom spoke these vows to each other:

I, [George/Kerry], take you, [Kerry/George], to be my [wife/husband], and in doing so, I commit my life to you. I embrace the sorrows and the joys, the hardships and the triumphs, and the experiences of our lives together. I promise to give as well as receive, to listen as well as speak, and to both respond and to inspire. I make this commitment in love.

Their ring exchange:

In token and pledge of my constant faith and abiding love, with this ring, I thee wed.

Celebrant:

These rings are the symbols of the vows here taken. They mark the beginning of a long journey together, filled with wonder, surprises, laughter, tears, celebration, grief, and joy. May these rings reflect the warmth of the lives that flow through them today. Two lives are now joined in one unbroken circle. Wherever they go, may they always return to one another. May they grow in understanding and in compassion. May the home that they establish be a place of peace, comfort, and sanctuary.

Do all those assembled affirm this marriage and give it your blessing? Please answer, "We do!"

I ask that everyone together please repeat after me, "We, your and friends, now pronounce you married!"

In the wedding celebration of Gino and Carol, the ceremony began with the Creation of the Circle, a pagan tradition that creates a bridge between the physical and spiritual worlds, forming a safe space in which the couple marry. The guardians of East, South, West, and North were invited in to bless the circle, and each member of the wedding party processed along its circumference, stopping at their place along the arc.

The perimeter was traced with rose petals as the flower girl took her turn around the ring. All who entered the circle were asked to come mindful of their commitment to this union, and the maid of honor and best man were each asked to pledge their support to the marriage. This couple included a handfasting in their celebration, and after declaring their willingness to enter into holy matrimony, spoke these vows, each in turn:

I, [Carol/Gino], take you [Gino/Carol], to be my [husband/wife]. You are the one I admire; you are the one I adore. You are the one I want to go on with forever, from now until the end of my life, wherever it leads. With gratitude that God has seen fit to bring us together, I promise to love you, honor you, and respect you, always.

Their ring exchange:

[Gino/Carol], wear this ring as a reminder that I love you every single day of your life. May it be the object that tells, when we as ourselves are no more and our bones have crumbled to dust, that our love in this life was real and eternal and deep.

Commitment Ceremonies

The only difference between a commitment ceremony and a "sanctioned" marriage ceremony is the recognition of an official authority. Craft your ceremony to reflect all the beautiful sentiment filling your hearts.

We affirm this day to become a family. We pledge to make time for each other, to bring to each other our true feelings, and be present with love and respect. We will stand side by side, understanding each other's weaknesses, creating a safe haven to explore and accept our differences. As we grow in our roles as lifelong partners, so will we always remain best friends. We make these promises this day, in front of all here present.

Vow Renewals

Annie and Kevin have created their own tradition, and renew their "contract" with each other every five years, rethinking and rewriting their promises to each other at every interval.

In view of our past and present happiness as partners in the enterprise of life, we resolve, in the company of these friends, to undertake a second term of five years' duration, in which span of time we will continue to encourage, honor, share, and entertain one another; to further our own and each other's understanding and appreciation of the larger world; and to remain fully conscious and disinterested in times, however momentary, of trial and difficulty. We seek to act with integrity in our relations with one another, to accept personal responsibility for our individual happiness and actions, and to use the strength we draw from one another to meet our broader challenges. We wish to provide for each other in the event of catastrophe, and to try at all times to help others. Foremost in our thoughts is the idea that this contract shall articulate our honest intentions toward each other and our desire to remain vigilant in adherence to these principles. To that end, this contract and this celebration will be renewed in five years' time.

Readings

Let me not to the marriage of true minds
Admit impediments. Love is not love

Which alters when it alteration finds

Or bends with the remover to remove.

O, no! it is an ever fixed mark,

That looks on tempests and is never shaken;

It is the star to every wand'ring bark,

Whose worth's unknown, although his height be taken.

Love's not Time's fool, though rosy lips and cheeks

Within his bending sickle's compass come;

Love alters not with his brief hours and weeks,

But bears it out even to the edge of doom.

If this be error and upon me prov'd,

I never writ, nor no man ever lov'd.

William Shakespeare

Love is patient, love is kind;

Love is not jealous or boastful;

it is never arrogant nor rude.

Love does not insist on its own way;

it is not irritable or resentful;

it does not rejoice at wrong,

but delights in the truth.

It is always ready to make allowances,

to trust, to hope,

and to endure whatever comes.

Love will never fail.

1 Corinthians 13:4–8

It is also good to love, because love is difficult. For one human being to love another is perhaps the most difficult task that has been entrusted to us, the ultimate task, the final test and proof, the work for which all other work is merely preparation. Love does not at first mean arousal, surrender, and uniting with another person—it is a high inducement for the individual to ripen, to become something in the inner self, to become mature in the outer world, to become world for the sake of another. This is a great, demanding claim on him, something that chooses him and calls him to vast distances.

Rainer Maria Rilke

Love is a great thing, a great good in every way; it alone lightens what is heavy, and leads smoothly over all roughness. For it carries a burden without being burdened, and makes every bitter thing sweet and tasty. Love wants to be lifted up, not held back by anything low. Love wants to be free, and far from all worldy desires, so that its inner vision may not be dimmed and good fortune bind it or misfortune cast it down. Nothing is sweeter than love.

Thomas à Kempis

And man and woman are like the earth, that brings forth flowers
in summer, and love, but underneath is rock.
Older than flowers, older than ferns, older than foraminiferæ,
older than plasm altogether is the soul of a man underneath.

And when, throughout all the wild orgasms of love
slowly a gem forms, in the ancient, once-more-molten rocks
of two human hearts, two ancient rocks, a man's heart and a woman's,
that is the crystal of peace, the slow hard jewel of trust,
the sapphire of fidelity.
The gem of mutual peace emerging from the wild chaos of love.

D.H. Lawrence

It seems to me, to myself,
that no man was ever before
to any woman what you are to me—
the fullness must be in proportion,
you know to the vacancy . . .
and only I know what was behind—
the long wilderness without the blossoming rose . . .
and the capacity for happiness,
like a black gaping hole,
before this silver flooding.

Elizabeth Barrett (Browning)

With thee conversing I forget all time,
All seasons and their change, all please alike.
Sweet is the breath of morn, her rising sweet,
With charm of earliest birds; pleasant the sun
When first on this delightful land he spreads
His orient beams, on herb, tree, fruit, and flower,
Glistring with dew; fragrant the fertile earth
After soft showers; and sweet the coming on
Of grateful evening mild, then silent night
With this her solemn bird and this fair moon,
And these the gems of heav'n, her starry train:
But neither breath of morn when she ascends
With charm of earliest birds, nor rising sun
On this delightful land, nor herb, fruit, flower,
Glistring with dew, nor fragrance after showers,
Nor grateful evening mild, nor silent night
With this her solemn bird, nor walk by moon,
Or glittering starlight without thee is sweet.

John Milton

33

Come live with me and be my love,
And we will all the pleasures prove
That valleys, groves, hills, and fields,
Woods, or steepy mountain yields.

And we will sit upon the rocks,
Seeing the shepherds feed their flocks,
By shallow rivers to whose falls
Melodious birds sing madrigals.

And I will make thee beds of roses
And a thousand fragrant posies,
A cap of flowers, and a kirtle
Embroidered all with leaves of myrtle;

A gown made of the finest wool
Which from our pretty lambs we pull;
Fair lined slippers for the cold,
With buckles of the purest gold;

A belt of straw and ivy buds,
With coral clasps and amber studs:
And if these pleasures may thee move,
Come live with me, and be my love.

The shepherds' swains shall dance and sing
For thy delight each May morning:
If these delights thy mind may move,
Then live with me and be my love.

Christopher Marlowe

The fountains mingle with the river
      And the rivers with the Ocean,
The winds of Heaven mix for ever
      With a sweet emotion;
Nothing in the world is single;
      All things by a law divine
In one spirit meet and mingle,
      Why not I with thine?—

See the mountains kiss high Heaven
      And the waves clasp one another;
No sister-flower would be forgiven
      If it disdained its brother;
And the sunlight clasps the earth
      And the moonbeams kiss the sea:
What is all this sweet work worth
      If thou kiss not me?

Percy Bysshe Shelley

I am my beloved's, and his desire is toward me.

Come, my beloved, let us go forth into the field;
let us lodge in the villages.

Let us wake early to the vineyards; let us see if the vine
flourish, whether the tender grape appear, and the
pomegranates bud forth: there will I give thee my loves.

The mandrakes give a smell, and at our gates are all
manner of pleasant fruits, new and old, which I have saved
for thee, my darling.

Song of Solomon 7:10–13

Entreat me not to leave thee, or to return from following after thee: for
whither thou goest, I will go; and where thou lodgest, I will lodge: thy
people shall be my people, and thy God my God:

Where thou diest, will I die, and there will I be buried: the Lord do so to me,
and more also, if ought but death part thee and me.

Ruth 1:16–17

If ever two were one, then surely we.

If ever man were loved by wife, then thee;

If ever wife was happy in a man,

Compare with me, ye women, if you can.

I prize thy love more than whole mines of gold

Or all the riches that the East doth hold.

My love is such that rivers cannot quench,

Nor ought but love from thee, give recompense.

Thy love is such I can no way repay,

The heavens reward thee manifold, I pray.

Then while we live, in love let's so persevere

That when we live no more, we may live ever.

Anne Bradstreet

Two are better than one; because they have a good reward for their labour.

For if they fall, the one will lift up his fellow: but woe to him that is alone when he falleth; for he hath not another to help him up.

Again, if two lie together then they have heat: but how can one be warm alone?

And if one prevail against him, two shall withstand him; and a threefold cord is not quickly broken.

Ecclesiastes 4:9–12

You were born together, and together you shall be forevermore.

You shall be together when the white wings of death scatter your days.

Ay, you shall be together even in the silent memory of God.

But let there be spaces in your togetherness,

And let the winds of the heavens dance between you.

Love one another, but make not a bond of love:

Let it rather be a moving sea between the shores of your souls.

Fill each other's cup but drink not from one cup.

Give one another of your bread but eat not from the same loaf.

Sing and dance together and be joyous, but let each one of you be alone,

Even as the strings of a lute are alone though they quiver with the same music.

Give your hearts, but not into each other's keeping.

For only the hand of Life can contain your hearts.

And stand together yet not too near together:

For the pillars of the temple stand apart,

And the oak tree and the cypress grow not

in each other's shadow.

Kahlil Gibran

Notes

Toasts

There are many occasions in life when lifting a glass and saying a few heartfelt words to celebrate an event or pay tribute to an honored guest is apropos. For centuries, toasts ranging from the short and sweet "Cheers!" to more elaborate and personalized addresses have been used to celebrate and commemorate the noteworthy: birthdays and anniversaries, births and graduations, new jobs and retirements. Perhaps one of the most touching moments in any wedding comes when a close friend or relative of the bride or groom rises to deliver an earnest toast in honor of the couple's new commitment.

What could be more elementary than the basic instructions for toasting: Stand up straight. Lift up your glass. Say something meaningful. Drink. But for many, thinking of something appropriate to say at such an important moment seems an impossible task. For others, the fear of speaking in public surpasses even the fear of dying. Relax! Breathe deeply. All you need to become an expert in this particular field is a little instruction, a little inspiration, and a little practice. Read on—help is on the way.

The Birth of a Toast

Today's modern toast can trace its lineage at least as far back as ancient Greece, when a typical method of dealing with one's enemies was to poison them during a "friendly" meal. The practice thus developed for the host to take the first drink of wine poured from a common vessel, to prove to the guest that the beverage was safe to consume. It became customary to accompany this first drink with a simple salute . . . "To your health!" Although this may seem a sinister origin for such a celebratory custom, centuries of civilization have tamed and refined it into the charming tradition we now know.

At most wedding receptions, the only person required to propose a toast is the best man. It is common, however, for his "official" wedding toast to be followed by salutations from any number of other people at the wedding, from the maid of honor and other attendants to the fathers and/or mothers of the bride and groom. At many weddings, any guest who feels moved to say a few words to favor the happy couple may do so. Even the bride and groom themselves might offer up a toast, to each

other, to their parents and new in-laws, to the members of the wedding party for their support, as well as to their honored guests.

The reception isn't the only wedding-related event where a glass will be lifted in praise. Engagement parties, the bachelor party, the bridesmaids' luncheon, and the rehearsal dinner will all be occasions for raised glasses and raised spirits. While this may seem like an overwhelmingly large number of public addresses on the same subject, one only has to remember that even a short sentiment qualifies as expert oratory if delivered with feeling.

Anatomy of a Toast

If you think you will be speaking, your first order of business is to think of something to say. A personalized speech is always the most meaningful, and the best place to start is to consider your relationship with the recipient of the toast. Are you the groom's older brother, or the bride's college roommate? Speak about the first lemonade stand that the two of you had, when the groom drank the entire pitcher before you could sell any of it. Tell of the bride's fondness for all-nighters on the eve of finals, or simply how you came to be friends. The story of how the couple met is always a favorite at weddings, and one that many of the guests may not know. Ask the bride's mother for her favorite memories of her daughter, and choose one that illustrates what you like best about her. Sharing an anecdote or memory is the perfect building block for a successful toast—even if it's someone else's!

Toasting Tips

Make sure your stories about the bride and groom are rated PG and are not overly embarrassing. Putting them on the hot seat with mild teasing is one thing, but humiliating them in front of their closest friends and family will not go over well with anyone.

If storytelling is not your style, share what this person means to you, or which attributes really distinguish his or her character. Does he call his parents on the first day of spring to ask if they need help installing the air conditioners? Is she the best Scrabble player you've ever met? Your audience has gathered to celebrate with the happy couple, and will be receptive to anything heartwarming you have to say about them. This is the perfect time to express emotion. Your sentiment does not need to be lengthy as long as it is spoken from your heart.

Once you have determined what the foundation of your toast will consist of, constructing it is a matter of putting one block atop the next. To get everyone's attention, you can start your toast with a little joke, an interesting quotation, or with a declaration of what you are about to do. Next, launch into the core of your toast: the story, memory, or idea you wish to share. Then get back to your purpose there, which is to congratulate the *couple*. If you have been speaking only about the bride, focus a moment of attention on the groom by saying it is clear that she has found her soul mate, or what a wonderful addition he makes to the family. Finally, conclude with a wish, blessing, or affectionate remark directed at both of them. Remember that a toast is always *to* someone or something. You may take a rambling path to get there, telling stories or jokes along the way, but ultimately you should come to the point, address the subjects of your toast, and end on a sincere note.

You may decide to say a few words to other participants at the wedding, to congratulate the parents or praise the bridal party, for example. This can add a certain charm to your toast, and it is a good idea to link this portion of your commentary back to the happy couple in some way. In this case, you can toast both parties, always ending with the newlyweds.

Toasting Tips

Humor is a great icebreaker in a toast. In entertaining your audience, you immediately relax them and warm them to whatever follows. However, humor can be tricky, so be sensitive, don't say anything that could be deemed offensive or off-color, and if there is any doubt, leave it out!

Special Delivery

Now that you know what you want to say, you have to concentrate on how you are going to say it. Take a tip from the Boy Scouts of America: be prepared. Jot down some notes or an outline of your toast on a piece of paper or index cards. The most successful toaster walks a fine line between being prepared and being overly rehearsed. This is not to say that you shouldn't practice your speech. On the contrary, the more you practice, the more familiar you'll become with the material. Consider practicing in front of someone else, or videotape yourself to get an idea of how others will see you. What you are striving for is to know your

speech well enough that you will remember it and be able to speak in a manner that sounds spontaneous, rather than having to read from a paper. If you are afraid that your mind will go blank at the critical moment, write out your speech verbatim and memorize it, but bring your notes in case you get stuck. If all else fails, read the contents of your toast to the crowd. As we've noted, this is a very forgiving audience. They are not there to judge your performance, but merely to hear what you have to say about someone they love. As long as you are earnest, they will applaud when you are finished.

Here's the good news—brevity is a virtue. Your toast should be no longer than three to five minutes, and can even be as short as one minute. You want to get your message across before your audience begins to wonder when the next course will be served.

Toasting Tips

A critical part of every toast is the drink, though it need not be an alcoholic beverage. Alert the master of ceremonies and/or catering staff before your toast, which will allow the guests the opportunity to refill their glasses.

Your big moment has come. It is always best to stand up when offering a toast, but if it's an intimate gathering and everyone can see you, it's acceptable to remain seated while speaking. The key here is that everyone should be able to see you, and you them. For the next few minutes, the spotlight will be on you. It is your job to smile broadly, stand (or sit) up straight, speak loudly and clearly, and exude confidence, no matter what you may be feeling at the moment. Resist the urge to rush through your speech. The honorees and guests really do want to hear what you have to say. And by all means, don't distract them. Fidgeting with your clothing, shifting from one foot to the other, injecting phrases such as "you know" or "like" or "ummm" will merely focus unneccessary attention on how nervous you are.

Toasting Tips

There should be a nearby surface on which you can set your notes or toasting glass, so that you don't have to juggle those two items along with the microphone.

As you begin to speak, remember to look around the room. Make eye contact with people in different areas. And by all means, from time to time look at the people you are honoring. When you are concluding your toast, look directly at the recipients as you express your tender wishes. Lift your glass to eye level, wait a brief moment to allow the guests to catch up to you, and take a

Toasting Tips

Unless you are a naturally dramatic person and completely comfortable speaking in front of people, don't try to be flamboyant. Speak in your normal voice and don't use unnatural hand gestures.

sip. Gather your notes and, with glass in hand, make a graceful exit. It would be a nice gesture to head over to the bride and groom for a quick hug and kiss before finding your seat. And just like that, your job is done!

Toasting Tips

If you are the one being toasted, etiquette states that you shouldn't raise your glass or drink from it during the toast itself. Once everyone else has taken a sip, you may then do so, or you may immediately counter with a toast of your own, taking a sip when you have finished.

So here's to you, dear reader. May your hands be steady, your heart steadfast, and your words inspired by divine revelation.

Inspiration

In the following sections, you will find actual toasts—short and long, poignant and playful, traditional and unconventional—to use as inspiration when creating your own toast. In addition, you'll find short quotations and poems to spark your imagination or spice up your material. It is important to note that many of the sentiments can be adapted to work in sections other than where they have been categorized, so be creative and move things around to fit your needs.

TO THE COUPLE

I am honored to have served as Steve's best man today, and thrilled to have the privilege to offer the first toast to the newlyweds. Ladies and gentlemen, please rise as we raise our glasses to Charla and Steve. May your lives together be long and filled with laughter, may you persevere and prosper, and may you always feel the joy you know today.

Where your pleasure is, there is your treasure: where your treasure, there your heart; where your heart, there your happiness.

Saint Augustine

I once heard a wonderful expression. "Love does not consist of gazing at each other, but in looking outward in the same direction," and I couldn't think of a more appropriate sentiment for this occasion. As I look at you both, sitting side by side gazing outward at all your friends and family, it is clear that you two have always been exactly so. You have always stood together as partners with the same ideals, the same goals, looking at the world around you and eager to see where it will take you. May you always move in the same direction, and each step bring you closer to your dreams.

There is nothing nobler or more admirable than when two people who see eye to eye keep house as man and wife, confounding their enemies and delighting their friends.

Homer

Patricia and James, fate has brought you together, and today you begin your lives anew. A toast to your future . . . may you take it one day at a time, and may it always be filled with great adventure. I love you both.

Write in your heart that every day is the best day of the year.

Ralph Waldo Emerson

Wishing you a lifetime of health and happiness.

ll love is sweet,

Given or returned. Common as light is love,

And its familiar voice wearies not ever . . . .

They who inspire it most are fortunate,

As I am now; but those who feel it most

Are happier still.

Percy Bysshe Shelley

May "for better or worse" be far better than worse.

Two souls with but a single thought,
Two hearts that beat as one.

Friedrich Halm

Welcome everyone. It's gratifying to see so many smiling faces shining for my son and new daughter-in-law. Watching my son grow into the man he is today has been the most rewarding experience of my life. I always wanted a daughter too, and tonight I know I have one. Frankly, if he hadn't given her the ring, I would have bought it myself. She's a very special person, and welcoming her into our family has been an honor and a privilege. She has made our lives complete. I always looked forward to the day when I would dance at my son's wedding, and tonight I will do so with a joyous heart. To you, my children, to the love you share with each other and your families. May it grow stronger with every passing day.

Marriage is the golden ring in a chain whose
beginning is a glance and whose ending is Eternity.

Kahlil Gibran

*Please join me as I propose a toast to our newlyweds: may you
have as much success in your new life together as you did in
finding true love. The best of luck to you, my friends.*

Render therefore to all their dues: tribute to whom
tribute is due; custom to whom custom; fear to
whom fear; honour to whom honour.

Owe no man anything, but to love one another:
for he that loveth another hath fulfilled the law.

Romans 13:7–8

Dear friends, may the sun shine brightly on your lives together. God bless you.

There is no more lovely, friendly and charming relationship, communion, or company than a good marriage.

Martin Luther

As you all know, Tony and Elizabeth have much in common . . . the same love affair with their computers, their ability to collect cats, and of course, their devotion to a few pop-culture science fiction genres. You also know that Tony and Elizabeth were friends for many years before their romance blossomed. I met them at exactly this turning point in their lives.

We were gathered for the vow renewal ceremony of our friends Annie and Kevin, and a group of us stayed together in their house. It was love at first sight, for me and Elizabeth and Tony. My own relationship with them has grown in these last few years, just as theirs has with each other. I felt privileged to witness the beginning of their fascination with each other, and am honored to have been here when they pledged their never-ending commitment to each other.

I have often attended weddings where I knew either the groom or the bride, but this is one of those special moments when I know and love them both, and knew from day one that these two were perfect for each other. To Tony and Elizabeth, may your love last well into the next Star Wars trilogy.

*Love consists in this, that two solitudes
protect and touch and greet each other.*

Rainer Maria Rilke

*I was delighted when Gino asked me to be his best man, and when he explained to
me that accepting the job would mean more than throwing him a bachelor party,
I was intrigued. He told me that the maid of honor and I would also be taking vows
during the ceremony . . . that we must be willing to pledge our support to their
marriage, to remind them of their promises to each other. And as I reflected on this
responsibility, I started thinking about the meaning of friendship. I thought of my
friendship with Gino, and how it has enriched my life. I thought of the added bonus
of developing a friendship with Carol. And I realized that a deep, intimate friendship is one of the most important things we can seek in this life. I'd like to read you
the words of Cicero, which perfectly reflect what I mean.*

    *"And so friendship is quite different from all the other things in the world on
which we are accustomed to set our hearts. In whatever direction you turn, it
still remains yours. No barrier can shut it out. It can never be untimely;
it can never be in the way. We need friendship all the time, just as much as
we need the proverbial necessities of life. And I am not speaking of ordinary,
commonplace friendships, delightful and valuable though they can be. What I
have in mind instead is the authentic, truly admirable sort of relationship, the*

sort that is embodied in those rare pairs of famous friends. When one thinks of a true friend, they are looking at themselves in a mirror. Friendship, then, both adds a brighter glow to prosperity and relieves adversity by dividing and sharing the burden. It is unique because of the bright rays of hope it projects into the future: and it never allows the spirit to falter or fall."

This is what I wish for the newlyweds in their lives together, that in addition to love, they also share authentic, profound friendship, and that this be their wedding present to each other. To Carol and Gino!

To the Bride or Groom

Friends and family, honored guests, today is the happiest day of my life so far. Today my darling daughter married a man I know to be worthy of her love. I know this because he and I spent many hours getting to know each other while they were dating.

You see, whenever he arrived to pick her up, she was usually still getting ready, a process that can take longer than painting the Brooklyn Bridge. But instead of just standing there, looking uncomfortable, Jack was always quite outgoing, not

to mention outspoken, and entangled me in conversation. You all know him, so you know what I mean by that! And I have to admit that in the beginning, I would have preferred if he tried to ingratiate himself by going out to the garage and waxing my car, so that I could watch television without his interruptions.

But that just isn't Jack's style, and in hindsight I'm grateful for it. As their romance blossomed, I came to know and love this young man very well. I learned what he believes in and whom he respects. I learned that he is hardworking and honest. I learned what he likes and what he dislikes . . . oh boy, did I hear a lot about what he dislikes! Above all, I learned how much he treasures my daughter, how much he values her opinions and admires her abilities, and how much he has come to love her. I am proud to have such a wonderful man as part of my family, and am indebted to my daughter for bringing him into our lives. Maya, the light that shines in my eyes when I look at you has just gotten brighter. To Maya and Jack: may you always bask in the glow of your love for each other."

Child of the pure, unclouded brow
And dreaming eyes of wonder!
Though time be fleet and I and thou
Are half a life asunder,
Thy loving smile will surely hail
The love-gift of a fairy tale.

Lewis Carroll

*Ladies and gentlemen, it has been my pleasure to know Sharon all her life, and
I felt deeply touched today as I witnessed their vows. I would like to propose a
traditional toast to the bride: to your health, happiness, and a joyous married life.*

Come. And be my baby.

Maya Angelou

831

8 letters . . . 3 words . . . 1 thought

I Love You

Beloved, think it not strange concerning the
fiery trial which is to try you, as though
some strange thing happened unto you.

1 Peter 4:12

Ladies and gentlemen, sometimes you know people for years, but you never really get close, you never really know each other. And then you meet someone like Robbin, who seemed to sense who I am the day we met. She loves me for myself, or maybe I should say, in spite of myself. And I love her for everything that she is, and everything that she will ever become. There is no doubt in my mind that we are for each other. In the words of Roy Croft, "I love you, not only for what you are, but for what I am when I am with you." To my bride: today we have joined our hearts with our futures. May we always be better than the sum of our parts, and may our love be more perfect than we can ever hope to be. I am so in love with you.

To love one maiden only, cleave to her,
And worship her by years of noble deeds,
Until they won her; for indeed I knew
Of no more subtle master under heaven
Than is the maiden passion for a maid,
Not only to keep down the base in man,
But teach high thought, and amiable words
And courtliness, and the desire of fame,
And love of truth, and all that makes a man.

Alfred, Lord Tennyson

Frank, I've never seen you happier than the day you met Lisa, until the day you realized you loved her. And I never saw you happier than you were that day, until the day you asked her to marry you, and she accepted. And I thought you couldn't be happier than that, but when I look at your face today, I see I was wrong, because today your happiness is so bright, it's blinding. May the two of you increase each other's joy in life, every day of your lives together.

Each friend represents a world in us, a world possibly not born until they arrive, and it is only by this meeting that a new world is born.

Anaïs Nin

I'm told that the best man's speech is traditionally directed to the bride, and I am delighted to preside over the only five minutes of the wedding that Bette did not plan! Yet I will tell you in all seriousness, just as she has been a force in bringing this wedding together, she has been a force in my life. Her friendship has influenced my life, not in an abstract way, but in some way more magical. If she and I weren't friends, I wouldn't be together with the woman that I love, and I wouldn't have the relationship that I now enjoy with the groom, a man who I'm proud to call my business partner and my best friend. By guiding me to these two most-beloved people on two seemingly ordinary days of my life, Bette changed the course of my life.

I imagine that this room is full of people who have a similar relationship with either the bride or the groom. This couple has affected us all. They have helped to shape our lives. And if we didn't know them, our lives might be completely different. We are gathered here today because we love them and they love each other, and that is what is really important on this earth. Bette, Antonio, as you begin your marriage, I offer you this. It's not your job to always agree with each other. It's not even your job to always understand each other. Your job, your only job, is to always love each other. To you!

One man in a thousand, Solomon says,
Will stick more close than a brother.
And it's worth while seeking him half your days
If you find him before the other.
Nine hundred and ninety-nine depend
On what the world sees in you,
But the Thousandth Man will stand your friend
With the whole round world agin you.

Rudyard Kipling

TO THE PARENTS

I've heard it is said that when a child finds true love, a parent finds true joy. May
you always know the joy you feel today, and may it grow ever greater with each
anniversary your children celebrate.

Experto credite.
Trust one who has gone through it.

Virgil

I can honestly say that I have never been to a more beautiful wedding, and certainly never one that touched me so deeply. I've spent many hours in your kitchen, and your company, over the years, sipping coffee and eating the best homemade oatmeal cookies I have ever tasted. I have watched the parade of your family life within those walls, and today I have watched the most radiant moment in that history. Seeing your faces as your daughter and her groom exchanged their promises just about moved me to tears. Thank you for allowing me to share this special moment in your lives. To our hosts, and to the joyous union of these two families.

appy he
With such a mother! Faith in womankind
Beats with his blood, and trust in all things high
Comes easy to him, and tho' he trip and fall
He shall not blind his soul with clay.

Alfred, Lord Tennyson

Ladies and gentlemen, my mother has been the guiding light in our family for our entire lives. She has loved us, provided for us, and taught us to value the things most important in life. My sister Maxine has learned much from my mother, and I'd like to tell you a story that illustrates this point. Shortly after they became engaged, Maxine and Joey were having a spirited teasing session about the differences between men and women. Joey came up with the ultimate example. He turned to me and asked, 'How many pairs of shoes do you think you own?' So I made a quick tally

in my head and gave him my answer, 'Four, maybe five.' 'See?' Joey said triumphantly to Maxine. 'Are you joking?' Maxine laughed, "I have more than that under my desk at work!" And so I'd like to propose a toast, ladies and gentlemen ... to my mother, whose closet rivals that of Imelda Marcos. She has taught us that compassion comes from walking in someone else's shoes, and that you can never get enough practice! And to the happy couple, may your triumphs in life be greater than the sum of Maxine's shoes, and may happiness never be more elusive than the nearest Kenneth Cole store."

The happiness of life is made up of minute fractions—the little soon-forgotten charities of a kiss or smile, a kind look, a heartfelt compliment, and the countless infinitesimals of pleasurable and genial feeling.

Samuel Taylor Coleridge

To the Wedding Party

Honored guests, it is a traditional wedding custom for the best man to proffer a toast to the bridesmaids on behalf of the bride and groom, and the groom has asked me to do just that. As their engagement progressed, the whirlwind of wedding activity surrounding these women could have fueled a nuclear submarine, concluding in a prewedding weekend that seemingly turned the happy couple's apartment into a sweat shop that would have surely brought law enforcement down upon them, had anyone been brave enough to inform them.

This morning I stopped in and thought I'd stepped into a battlefield. Clad in jeans and T-shirts, ponytails and bandannas, they were a motley crew . . . the frantic pace in that house as they worked was overwhelming. They appeared to each be doing five things at once. Flowers and ribbons flew through the air, and the constant sound of clippers and hammers and I don't know what else kept up an underlying beat by which they paced themselves.

I was frightened. I returned to my little male world, where we sat around scratching ourselves until it was time to dress. And I was amazed to see these same women, a mere hour or two later, wafting down the aisle, transformed, unfazed, perfectly poised, and radiating elegance. I stand in awe, ladies and gentlemen, and would ask you to rise as well. Out of love and devotion, these talented women turned the bride's vision into a realized dream. They have stamped a personalized touch on this celebration, and they have done so with the revelry that exists between friends. And so a toast to this wonderful support group, may you always know that what your heart gives away is kept in the hearts of others, and may the happiness you have brought to our newlyweds come back to you tenfold.

A happy bridesmaid makes a happy bride.
Alfred, Lord Tennyson

George Eliot wrote, "What do we live for if not to make the world less difficult for each other?" Today, and every day that we have known you all, you have eased our burdens. We thank you for your support, and look forward to a lifetime of paying you back.

Tell me what company thou keepest,
and I'll tell thee what thou art.

Miguel de Cervantes

We would like to thank each of you for sharing this day with us. We feel blessed to have every one of you in our lives. May the community we call family and friends continue to grow and thrive, and may every celebration in your lives shine with the light you have added to ours.

Make happy those who are near,
and those who are far will come.

Chinese Proverb

I've heard that happiness is the road traveled in the company of those you relish. As I look at my charming husband, I must be the happiest woman alive right now, all the more so because I see it reflected in all of your eyes. Thank you for traveling with us. May all your hopes and dreams come true, as mine have today.

Finally, brethren, farewell. Be perfect, be of good comfort, be of one mind, live in peace; and the God of love and peace shall be with you.

Greet one another with an holy kiss.

All the saints salute you.

2 Corinthians 13:11—13

Prewedding Toasts

To my bride and her family, who will soon be mine as well, you have believed in me and helped me to believe that even the impossible is possible. Eleanor Roosevelt said, "The future belongs to those who believe in their dreams." Tomorrow my dreams will come true. May this glass never be used for a less worthy cause than to drink to your good fortune and our future together.

For nothing worthy proving can be proven,
Nor yet disproven: wherefore thou be wise,
Cleave ever to the sunnier side of doubt.

Alfred, Lord Tennyson

I'd like to make a toast to the groom, may
this be your last solo gig ever.
(The recipient of this toast was a musician)

This is the day the Lord has made,
Let us rejoice and be glad in it!

Psalms 118:24

Notes

Index

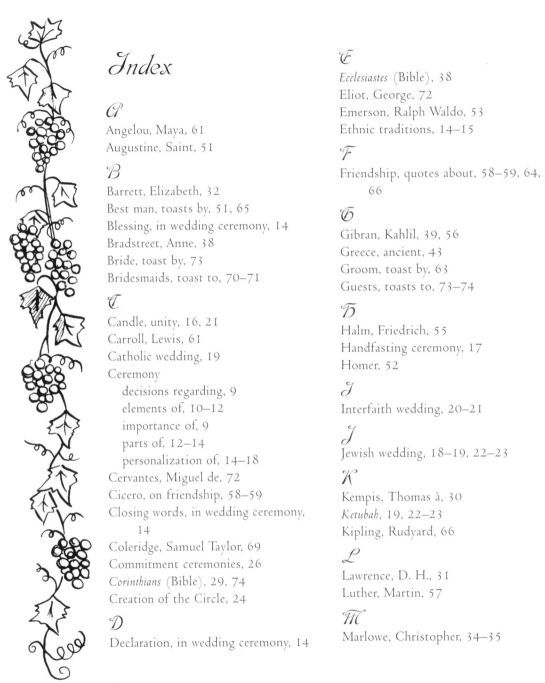

Further Reading

Fox, Rosemary (Illustrator). *Treasury of Wedding Poems, Quotations, and Short Stories.* New York: Hippocrene Books, 1998.

Glusher, David, and Peter Misner. *Words for the Wedding: The Wedding Service Book.* San Francisco, CA: Harper Press, 1994.

Hass, Robert, and Stephen Mitchell (Eds.). *Into the Garden: A Wedding Anthology.* New York: Harperperrenial Library: 1994.

Keeler-Evans, Ann. *Promises to Keep: Crafting Your Wedding Ceremony.* Emerald Earth Publishers, 2001.

Kigma, Daphne Rose. *Weddings from the Heart: Contemporary and Traditional Ceremonies for an Unforgettable Wedding.* Conari Press, 1995.

Lluch, Elizabeth, and Alex Lluch. *The Indispensable Groom's Guide.* Wedding Solutions Press, 1997.

Matthews, Bette. *The Wedding Workbook.* New York: Friedman/Fairfax Publishers, 1999.

McCluskey, John William. *The Complete Book of Wedding Toasts.* Arden Books, 2000.

Munro, Eleanor C. (Ed.). *Wedding Readings: Centuries of Writings and Rituals on Love and Marriage.* New York: Penguin USA, 1996.

Nelson, Gertrude Mueller, and Christopher Witt. *Sacred Threshold: Rituals and Readings for a Wedding with Spirit.* New York: Doubleday Books, 1998.

Paris, Wendy, and Andrew Chesler. *Words for the Wedding.* Perigee Press, 2001.

Post, Peggy. *Wedding Etiquette.* New York: Harper Resource, 2001.

Roney, Carley. *The Knot Guide to Wedding Vows and Traditions: Readings, Rituals, Music, Dances, Speeches, and Toasts.* New York: Broadway Books, 2000.

Ross-MacDonald, Jane. *Alternative Weddings: An Essential Guide for Creating Your Own Ceremonies.* Dallas, TX: Taylor Publishing, 1997.

Stewart, Arlene Hamilton. *A Bride's Book of Wedding Traditions.* New York: Hearst Books, 1995.

Warner, Diane. *Complete Book of Wedding Vows.* Franklin Lakes, NJ: Career Press, 1996.

Weinert, Fifi. *Best-Loved Wedding Traditions.* California: Andrews and McMeel, 2000.

Yager, Cary O. *The Bride's Book of Poems.* Chicago, IL: Contemporary Publishing, 1995.

Younkin, Marty. *A Wedding Ceremony to Remember: Perfect Words for the Perfect Wedding.* Love Notes Press, 2000.